A Note to Parents and Teachers

Eyewitness Readers is a compelling new reading programme for children. *Eyewitness* has become the most trusted name in illustrated books, and this new series combines the highly visual *Eyewitness* approach with engaging, easy-to-read stories. Each *Eyewitness Reader* is guaranteed to capture a child's interest while developing his or her reading skills, general knowledge and love of reading.

The books are written by leading children's authors and are designed in conjunction with literacy experts, including Cliff Moon M.Ed., Honorary Fellow of the University of Reading. Cliff Moon spent many years as a teacher and teacher educator specializing in reading. He has written more than 140 books for children and teachers, and he reviews regularly for teachers' journals.

The four levels of *Eyewitness Readers* are aimed at different reading abilities, enabling you to choose the books that are exactly right for each child.
Level 1 – Beginning to read
Level 2 – Beginning to read alone
Level 3 – Reading alone
Level 4 – Proficient readers

The "normal" age at which a child begins to read can be anywhere from three to eight years old, so these levels are only general guidelines. No matter which level you select, you can be sure that you're helping children learn to read, then read to learn!

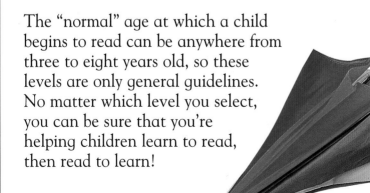

www.dk.com

Editor Dawn Sirett
Art Editor Jane Horne

Senior Editor Linda Esposito
Senior Art Editor
Diane Thistlethwaite
Production Melanie Dowland
Picture Researcher Andrea Sadler
Jacket Designer Margherita Gianni
Illustrator Gill Tomblin
Specially commissioned photography
Steve Gorton

Reading Consultant
Cliff Moon, M.Ed.

Published in Great Britain by
Dorling Kindersley Limited
9 Henrietta Street
London WC2E 8PS

2 4 6 8 10 9 7 5 3

Eyewitness Readers™ is a trademark of
Dorling Kindersley Limited, London.

A CIP catalogue record for this book is
available from the British Library.

ISBN 0-7513-598-58

Colour reproduction by Colourscan, Singapore
Printed and bound in Belgium by Proost

The publisher would like to thank the following for
their kind permission to reproduce their photographs:
Key: a=above, t=top, b=bottom, l=left, r=right, c=centre

Images Colour Library: 10 c, 32 clb; **NASA:** 20 cb, 32 cra;
NHPA: 17 br, 32 tr; **Oxford Scientific Films:** W. S. Pike 27 cb,
32 crb, Warren Faidley 14 clb, 32 bl; **Pictor International:** 6 br,
6 tc, 28 c, 32 cla, 32 br; **Science Photo Library:** Claude
Nuridsany/Marie Perennou 2 tr, 5 cl, 5 b, 32 tl; Mehau
Kulyk 5 tr; **Tony Stone Images:** front cover background.

Additional credits:
Jane Burton, Daniel Pangbourne, Kim Taylor (additional
photography for DK); Paul Scannell (window frame
model maker). The publisher would also like to thank
Andrew Krag for appearing in this book.

EYEWITNESS READERS

BEGINNING
1
TO READ

Whatever the
Weather

Written by Karen Wallace

London • New York • Sydney • Delhi

William watches from the window.
It's cold outside.
Snow is falling.
Each tiny snowflake
is made of ice.

snowflake

William watches from the window
Icicles shine in the trees.
Icicles form when
drops of water drip
then freeze and stick together.

icicles

William watches from the window.

Today it's warm.

The snow is slushy.

Icicles melt and turn to water.

They drip, drop, drip, drop
to the ground.

William watches from the window
Trees are bending in the wind.
Wind is air that's always moving.
Wind blows clouds across the sky.

clouds

William watches from the window.
He hears the wind
scream and whistle.
He sees a tree bend over double.
S~N~A~P~!
A big branch breaks in two!

William's safe and warm inside.

William watches from the window

He watches storm clouds
fill the sky.

ZAp!

He sees a flash of lightning.

BOOM!

He hears the thunder rumble.

William holds his teddy near him.

lightning

William watches from the window.
Rain drops freeze.
They turn to hailstones.
Hailstones clatter on the glass.
Some are as small as
apple pips.
Some are as big as
cherry stones.

hailstones

William watches from the window.
The stormy clouds
have blown away.
Fluffy clouds float in the sky.
Fluffy clouds mean better weather.

William watches from the window
The sun is hot.
The glass feels warm.
He knows the sun is a ball of fire
far away in outer space.

sun

William watches from the window.
Dark clouds are coming.
They are full of rain drops.
Soon the sky is grey again.

William watches from the window
He watches raindrops
plop and splatter.
William keeps his fingers crossed.
He's hoping it will rain and rain.

William watches from the window.
Rain is pouring from the sky.
It soaks the ground and
lies in puddles.

William smiles …

puddle

Teddy watches by the window.
A rainbow glitters in the sky.
William's outside in the sunshine.

What is William doing?

rainbow

SPLASH!

William is jumping into puddles!

SPLOSH!

His boots are shiny and new!

SPLISH! SPLASH! SPLOSH!

Jumping in and out of puddles

is William's favourite thing to do!

Picture Word List

snowflake
page 5

hailstones
page 17

icicles
page 6

sun
page 20

clouds
page 10

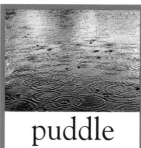
puddle
page 27

lightning
page 14

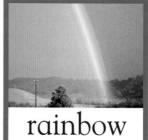
rainbow
page 28